What NOT to Do at Your Wedding!

What NOT to Do at Your Wedding!
Copyright © 2006 Sweetwater Press
Produced by Cliff Road Books

All rights reserved. No part of this book may be reproduced in any form or by any electronic or mechanical means, including information storage and retrieval systems, without written permission of the publisher.

Printed in The United States of America

ISBN-13: 978-1-58173-513-0
ISBN-10: 1-58173-513-8

Cover design by Miles G. Parsons

This work is a compilation from numerous sources. Every effort has been made to ensure accuracy. However, the publisher cannot be responsible for incorrect information.

What NOT to Do at Your Wedding!

Compiled and Edited by
Linda J. Beam

About the Author

Linda J. Beam holds a B.A. in English from Judson College, and an M.A. in English from the University of Alabama at Birmingham. Her extensive editorial experience includes work with medical journals and textbooks, and a variety of corporate publications. In addition, she has developed and presented business communication seminars on business writing, and basic grammar and punctuation. She currently works as Managing Editor at Crane Hill Publishers in Birmingham, Alabama.

Other works by Linda include *What NOT to Say!*, *What NOT to Name Your Baby!*, *What NOT to Do in Polite Company!*, *What NOT to Do at Work!*, *What NOT to Do in Love!*, *What NOT to Do When you Graduate!*, and *What's Your Bible I.Q.?*

Contents

After You Say "Yes"! 7

Starting at the Beginning: Getting a Game Plan 9

The Wedding Party: Etiquette for an Exclusive Entourage 19

Blending Your Families: Reckoning with Relatives Respectfully 33

What to Wear: All about Attire 39

All That Glitters Is Not Gold: Rules for Rings and Things 51

Decorating for the Ceremony: Featuring Flowers with Flair 61

Let Them Eat Cake: Conquering Catering Concerns 67

Picture This: Preparing for Perfect Photographs 73

Melodies for Marriage: Making the Most of Your Music 81

Be Our Guest: The Ins and Outs of Invitations 87

Showers and Other Get-togethers: Pointers for Prenuptial Parties 95

Setting up Housekeeping: Getting Gifts Graciously 101

Let's Call the Whole Thing Off: Canceling with Consideration 109

Now I Pronounce You: Conducting the Ceremony Correctly 115

Receiving Your Guests: Recipe for a Ritzy Reception 123

Getting Away from It All: Honeymooning without Hassles 131

Tying up Loose Ends: Finishing with Finesse 137

After You Say "Yes"!

Ask anyone who's ever been married and they'll tell you that making the decision to get married is the easy part. Handling all the details of arranging the wedding is more difficult. Fun, yes. Scary, sure. Exciting, definitely. But daunting, too. There are hundreds of details to keep track of, and many decisions to be made along the way. It's no wonder that many couples want to chuck the whole thing and elope before the big day.

It doesn't have to be overwhelming, though. You can have the wedding of your dreams, things can go as planned, and you can have wonderful memories to cherish. It just can't be done without effort.

That's where this book comes in. It offers guidelines on just about every aspect of a wedding you can think of to let you know ahead of time what to expect, what to dodge, and how to handle things when problems arise. It's sure to be a valuable reference for getting you to your big day in style.

Starting at the Beginning: Getting a Game Plan

Starting at the Beginning: Getting a Game Plan

There are many details involved in making a wedding a success, and careful attention should be paid to all of them, big and small. Begin by getting an overview of all the tasks ahead of you.

What NOT to Do

- Do not try to please others by doing your wedding as they suggest. It's your wedding. Do it your way.

- Do not make major decisions without consulting your fiancé(e).

- Do not discuss the particulars of your budget with other people. Unless they are helping to finance the event, the details are not their concern.

- Do not expect service providers to work for unreasonably low prices. Get the best deals you can, but be willing to pay appropriately for people's time and efforts.

> "Of all actions of a man's life, his marriage does least concern other people; yet of all actions of our life, 'tis most meddled with by other people."
> — John Selden

- Do not forget to allow yourself time for rest, relaxation, and lighter moments during the intensity of planning your wedding.

- Do not expect that everything will go perfectly. There are bound to be glitches, but you can deal with them.

- Do not make spur-of-the moment decisions about anything. Take time to consider everything carefully.

Starting at the Beginning: Getting a Game Plan

- Do not be rigid with your plans. Try to be flexible when possible.

- Do not spend so much on the wedding that you enter your new marriage heavily in debt.

- Do not make unreasonable demands of the people helping you make your plans.

- Do not use your wedding as a time to highlight and perpetuate family differences.

- Do not allow differences of opinion about wedding details to come between you and your fiancé(e).

- Do not neglect your relationship with your fiancé(e) as you get caught up in planning the wedding.

> **About one-half of all brides enlist the help of a wedding consultant or coordinator to help make their big day perfect.**

What to Do

- Leave enough time to handle all the details.

- Allow for the unexpected.

- Remember that the marriage is the most important thing, not the wedding.

- Take advantage of a professional wedding planner if possible. It will take some of the burden off your shoulders, and will leave you time to deal with other details that only you can handle.

- Ask professionals who will be helping you how much time they will need to get everything done properly.

Starting at the Beginning: Getting a Game Plan

- Select a date for your wedding that is not already notable for something else. Obvious dates to avoid would be Friday the 13th, April 1, September 11, and Daylight Saving Time transition days, which might be confusing to guests.

- Choose attendants and other members of the wedding party with care. They will be part of your memories of your special day, and will be a part of the photos that you will cherish.

> A thoughtful and useful pre-wedding gift to your attendants is a small calendar with all the important wedding-related activities already inked in on the appropriate dates.

- Try to choose outfits that your attendants really can wear later.

- Get details in writing. There is nothing worse than thinking you are getting a particular product or service in one way, and finding out that you are incorrect.

- Keep receipts for everything you pay for in connection to the wedding.

- Select some method of keeping all your details organized. Many people use index cards, and some find a loose leaf notebook system helpful.

- List all wedding tasks to be done and assign a due date for each. This will be helpful when meeting with suppliers of goods and services.

- Find out deadlines by which you will have to have particular decisions made and abide by them. They are intended to help you.

Starting at the Beginning: Getting a Game Plan

- Get a master calendar where all activities, plans, and deadlines will be recorded.

- Begin to think about what type of service you would like, what traditions you would like to honor, and what religious elements you would like to include.

- Have a back-up plan if your wedding is planned for outdoors.

> Some couples keep family and friends apprised of their wedding plans by creating their own personal websites that offer updates as the big day gets closer.

- As you begin to think of whom you will invite, keep a list of extras that out-of-town guests will need, such as a ride to the rehearsal dinner.

- Enlist help ahead of time to help accommodate special needs of guests.

- Be ready to bear the expense of extras that you ask your attendants to have, such as professionally applied make-up or perfect manicures.

> Our culture has a new term for brides who become difficult and demanding during the planning of their fairytale day: bridezilla. This combination of bride and Godzilla is characterized by a bride's overwhelming drive to create the perfect day, and to walk over anyone or anything to obtain it.

Starting at the Beginning: Getting a Game Plan

- Check well ahead of the wedding for marriage license requirements.

- Plan to show your appreciation to members of the wedding party with a gift to help commemorate the occasion.

- Send thank-you notes promptly so you do not feel overwhelmed by the task.

- Take time to enjoy the journey to the altar. Relax and savor the process.

- Begin to develop a budget for your wedding expenses.

- Include in the budget honorariums for the minister, musicians, and others who help with the ceremony but who are not attendants.

- Decide up front who will pay for what. There are traditional guidelines about this, though in recent years they have become more casual. Here are some suggestions about this important facet of planning a wedding:

> The average cost of a wedding is $20,000 to $25,000. It is expected to top $30,000 by 2010.

Bride's Family
- Bridal brunch
- Bridesmaids' luncheon
- Church fees
- Decorative items for the church and reception
- Flowers for church, bridesmaids, and reception

Starting at the Beginning: Getting a Game Plan

- Gifts for the bridal party
- Groom's gift
- Groom's ring
- Janitorial workers
- Lodging for bridesmaids, if necessary
- Lodging for out-of-town guests
- Musician fees for the ceremony and reception
- Printed items such as invitations, programs, napkins, and wedding novelties
- Reception costs
- Rice bags
- Wedding breakfast
- Wedding cake
- Wedding gown, headpiece, and accessories
- Wedding photos and videos

Groom's family

- Bride's bouquet
- Bride's gift
- Bride's ring
- Boutonnieres for groomsmen and ushers
- Clergy fees
- Gifts for groomsmen
- Groom's cake
- Honeymoon arrangements

Starting at the Beginning: Getting a Game Plan

> **Many couples have found that a good way to offset wedding expenses is by having sponsors pay for their weddings. Between radio and TV contests that coordinate and then broadcast the wedding, and local businesses willing to offer goods and services for a bit of advertising, lucky couples can have their dream wedding at little or no cost.**

- Limousine service for the bride and groom
- Lodging for groomsmen, if necessary
- Marriage license
- Mother's corsages
- Rehearsal dinner

Bridal party
- Bridesmaid dress
- Gift for the couple
- The shower
- Transportation

Groomsmen
- Bachelor party
- Gift for the couple
- Tuxedo or suit
- Transportation

The Wedding Party: Etiquette for an Exclusive Entourage

The Wedding Party:
Etiquette for an Exclusive Entourage

The wedding party is an important feature of the wedding. Here are some considerations as you begin to think about who should be part of this select group.

CHOOSING THE WEDDING PARTY

Choose your wedding party carefully because it will be comprised of people who will help you through the days of planning, and then will be an integral part of memories of your special day.

What NOT to Do

- Do not take the choice of your wedding party lightly. These are the people who will see you through all the ups and downs of planning for your big day, and who will stand with you as you make one of the most important commitments of your life.

- Do not yield to pressure to include people whom you would rather not have in your wedding party.

- Do not feel guilty for not including people that you choose not to have in the party.

- Do not choose people that you cannot rely on. You'll need to count on your wedding party to take care of some things on their own, and you do not need to choose people you will have to check up on.

- Do not be hurt if people you ask to be in the party decline. There may be issues about expense and availability that you are not aware of.

- Do not have attendants meet for the first time at rehearsal, particularly those who will walk down the aisle or stand together in

The Wedding Party:
Etiquette for an Exclusive Entourage

the ceremony. Offer an opportunity before the rehearsal for everyone to meet and get to know each other.

What to Do

- Decide how many attendants you will have. Many of your decisions will be based on this number.

- Keep size in mind. More attendants mean more expense, more opinions to consider, and more people to coordinate.

- Find other jobs for people who had hoped to be in the wedding party, but who were not chosen. For example, you'll need someone to keep the guest book, and someone to handle gifts.

- Include people from both sides of the family as attendants.

- Consider non-traditional choices for honor attendants. Siblings and friends of either gender may participate in any way you choose.

Attendants for a traditional Moroccan wedding have more to do than just agree on dresses. Five days before the wedding, they supervise the bride as she is bathed, has make-up applied to her hands and feet, and is dressed in white embroidered robes. The next evening, they carry the bride, who is sitting on a round table, on their shoulders to the bridal chamber as they sing and shout. After this, they remain behind a screen in the bridal chamber to verify her virginity and witness consummation of the marriage. Then they give the bride a second ritual bath, and finally leave the couple alone.

The Wedding Party:
Etiquette for an Exclusive Entourage

- Let all members of the party know the particulars of the wedding: date, time, and what you would like them to do in connection with your wedding.

- Offer updates as plans progress.

- Remember to express your appreciation to members of the wedding party with a gift or token of your thanks. Usually these are given at the rehearsal dinner.

- Include all members and their spouses or dates at the rehearsal dinner.

- Send thank-you notes to members of the wedding party when you return from your honeymoon.

RESPONSIBILITIES OF THE WEDDING PARTY

Being selected to be part of the wedding party is not just an honor — there are specific things expected of each person chosen. Here are some general responsibilities of people in the wedding party.

What NOT to Do

- Do not act like your concerns are the most important consideration. The focus should be on the bride and groom's preferences.

- Do not be upset if decisions are made that are not what you would have chosen.

- Do not relay to the bride or groom unkind comments or dissension among the wedding party members. If there is a problem, let the people involved work it out.

The Wedding Party:
Etiquette for an Exclusive Entourage

- Do not agree to be in the wedding party without understanding everything that will be expected of you.

- Do not balk at responsibilities that you have already agreed to.

> "Here's to matrimony, the high sea for which no compass has yet been invented!"
> Heinrich Heine

- Do not drop out of the wedding after agreeing to be in it unless extreme circumstances demand it.

What to Do
- Express to the bride and groom how much you appreciate being included in their plans.

- Work with the bride and groom to help make their plans a reality.

- Stay in touch with the bride and groom and be current on wedding plans.

- Understand what will be expected of you as a member of the wedding party before you agree to participate. This includes time and money involved.

- Take care of responsibilities normally assigned to members of the wedding party as listed below.

Father of the Bride
- Pay for the wedding unless the bride is already financially independent and prefers to pay for it herself.

- Take the bride from her home to the wedding site.

- Arrive at the site early enough to be available for scheduled photographs.

The Wedding Party:
Etiquette for an Exclusive Entourage

- Escort the bride down the aisle to the altar during the ceremony.

- "Give the bride away" if she would like to include this traditional part of the wedding ceremony.

- Receive guests at the reception, along with the bride's mother, the groom's parents, and other party members the bride wishes to include.

> In Russia, it's a tradition for the bride's mother to give the newlyweds a loaf of bread at their wedding reception. Whoever can take the largest bite becomes the head of the household. Usually this is to the man's advantage.

- Offer a toast to the couple at the reception or post-wedding dinner.

Mother of the Bride

- Be a source of support for the bride as she sorts out her plans.

- See that the bride's wishes are carried out on every detail of the wedding.

- Help the bride and groom decide on a wedding budget, but only if asked.

- Help the bride select her wedding attire.

- Coordinate the guest lists of the bride's side, as well as the groom's. The list must be complete before invitations can be ordered.

- Attend prenuptial parties and showers.

- Make reservations for out-of-town guests invited by the bride's family.

The Wedding Party:
Etiquette for an Exclusive Entourage

- Choose a gown for the wedding and immediately tell the mother of the groom so she can make her selection in a complimentary color.

- Spread the word about where the couple is registered for wedding gifts.

- Help with logistics such as seating plans for the reception and receiving line organization.

Father of the Groom

- Serve as the best man, if asked.

- Read Scripture or help with lighting a special candle during the ceremony if requested.

- Host the after-rehearsal dinner, along with the groom's mother.

- Join other parents of the bride and groom in the receiving line to greet guests.

Mother of the Groom

- Initiate contact with the groom's family if the two families have not met yet.

- Provide an accurate guest list, keeping in mind the number set by the bride's family.

- Choose a gown of complimentary color after the bride's mother has first chosen hers.

- Make reservations for out-of-town guests on the groom's guest list.

- Host the rehearsal dinner. Work with the bride and groom to determine how simple or elegant they would like this to be, and what kind of food they prefer.

The Wedding Party:
Etiquette for an Exclusive Entourage

- Arrive before the wedding in time to be included in photographs.

- Attend prenuptial parties and showers.

- Participate in the ceremony if asked to do so. Some mothers of grooms are asked to participate in some small way in the ceremony, such as by lighting a candle.

- Stand in the receiving line to introduce friends and family to the bride and her family.

Maid/Matron of Honor

- Attend all prenuptial parties.

- Help address invitations and announcements, make rice bags, etc.

- Sponsor a party for the bride and groom.

- Be sure that bridesmaids are kept aware of all pre-wedding details.

> Having both a maid and matron of honor is becoming a popular trend. Just be sure to make decisions early on about practical matters such as who will stand nearer the bride at the altar, and who will help the bride with her dress, bouquet, and ring.

- Help the bride pack for the honeymoon.

- Arrive early enough before the wedding to help with last minute details, as well as to be in scheduled photographs.

- Assist the bride with arranging her dress before she enters the church, during the ceremony, and during the reception.

- Help the bride with her bouquet as needed during the ring portion of the ceremony.

The Wedding Party:
Etiquette for an Exclusive Entourage

- Assist the photographer with identification of family members who should be included in poses.

> "A happy bridesmaid makes a happy bride."
> Alfred, Lord Tennyson

- Witness and sign the marriage certificate.

- Stand in the receiving line if asked by the bride to do so.

- See that the bride's gown is taken care of after she leaves.

Best Man

- Make sure that the groom has the marriage license at the wedding.

- Take care of any pre-wedding arrangements that the groom may delegate to him.

- Help the groom pack for the honeymoon.

- Get the minister's fee from the groom and see that the minister gets it after the ceremony.

- Carry the bride's ring until needed in the ceremony.

- Arrange to have the bride and groom's luggage ready to leave for the honeymoon.

Although many wedding parties include a child who serves as the ring bearer, it is usually best for the best man to keep the actual ring. Children given this responsibility sometimes do not make it down the aisle due to stage fright, and may even drop the ring.

The Wedding Party:
Etiquette for an Exclusive Entourage

> **UglyDress.com advertises itself as "the archive of the world's worst bridesmaids dresses." Some of the samples featured include "The Flat Chest Dress," "The Pregnant Prom Dress," and one they call "Married in a Whorehouse."**

- Ride to the church with the groom.
- Make sure the ushers are together and ready before the wedding.
- Make sure the groom has all the proper travel documents before the honeymoon.
- Make sure the groom has the proper currency if the honeymoon is to be abroad.
- Witness and sign the marriage certificate.
- Offer the first toast to the bride and groom at the reception.

> **Junior bridesmaids are usually girls (aged 9-14) that are too old to be flower girls but too young to be regular bridesmaids. They usually wear dresses similar, if not like, the bridesmaids', and besides being in the wedding party, they may help hand out programs, bubbles, and rice bags at the service.**

- Help make guests feel at home at the reception, and offer directions when asked.
- Return the groom's tuxedo to the tux shop after the ceremony.

The Wedding Party:
Etiquette for an Exclusive Entourage

Bridesmaids

- Offer to help with pre-wedding tasks. This could include making rice bags, or giving an out-of-town guest a ride from the airport the day of the wedding.

- Help plan, co-host, and pay for the bachelorette party/shower with the other bridesmaids.

- Attend the rehearsal and rehearsal dinner.

- Keep abreast of and participate in all wedding-related activities.

> Flower girls are young girls (aged 3-8) who proceed down the aisle just before the bride, scattering rose petals along the bridal path.

- Help introduce reception guests to each other, and make sure everyone knows the location of such places as the bar and restrooms.

- Encourage guest interaction at the reception by helping to get dancing started, and even offering to dance with guests as needed.

- Help the bride as needed with tasks such as freshening her make-up for pictures or carrying her train.

- Stand in the receiving line if asked by the bride to do so.

- Offer emotional support to the bride when preparations are intense prior to the wedding, and on the wedding day, when nerves are on edge.

Groomsmen

- Join together with the best man to prepare a bachelor party.

- Plan only activities that will be in good taste and will not offend the groom or parents of the couple.

The Wedding Party:
Etiquette for an Exclusive Entourage

- Participate in pre-wedding activities such as parties, the rehearsal, and the post-rehearsal dinner.

- Offer advice when asked to do so by the groom.

> During the time of marriage by capture, friends of the groom-to-be helped him kidnap his bride from her family. The first ushers and best man may have been like a small army fighting off angry relatives.

- Get to the wedding site in time to be available for scheduled photographs of the party.

- Seat guests as they arrive at the ceremony.

- Arrive early enough to be ready to seat even early birds.

- Pass out programs and other items as needed at the wedding.

- Dance with bridesmaids and other guests at the reception.

- Offer a toast or speech at the reception if it is appropriate.

Blending Your Families: Reckoning with Relatives Respectfully

Blending Your Families:
Reckoning with Relatives Respectfully

Millions of jokes have been made about the relationship between couples and their in-laws, and for good reason. As the wedding approaches, here are two sets of parents, each loving their own child and wanting the best for him or her. But sometimes good intentions take a wrong turn. Here are some ways to lay the groundwork for good relationships with your new family members.

What NOT to Do

- Do not expect your new family members to act and think the same as you do. They probably won't.

- Do not expect your fiancé(e) to share your opinion about his or her family.

- Do not prefer one set of parents over the other in making wedding plans.

- Do not talk negatively about your in-laws to other people. Observe the adage that if you can't say anything nice, don't say anything.

- Do not call your in-laws by their first names or by other familiar terms without asking if they mind.

The Society for Tortured Daughter-In-Laws is a website for women unhappy with their mother-in-laws. Welcoming new members by asking the question, "So you gave up your last name and all you got was a lousy mother-in-law?" the site claims that "We know your situation. We've all lived through it." It offers a Rant Zone for topics like "Worst Gifts" and "The Worst Thing She Ever Said."

Blending Your Families: Reckoning with Relatives Respectfully

- Do not allow any parent's opinion to weigh more heavily in a couple's decisions than the couple's.

- Do not expect relatives who work in wedding-related jobs to provide goods and services at no cost.

- Do not allow family disagreements to spill over into the wedding. It will be stressful enough without extra issues.

- Do not make plans for relatives who do not care for each other to handle any wedding-related task together.

- Do not allow small grievances to fester into larger ones. Ignore what you can, or confront issues and settle them. Decide which issues really won't matter in the long run.

> In early frontier days, courting often took place within the confines of one-room cabins. Parents indicated approval of their daughter's beau by making an early exit and leaving the couple alone. If they disapproved of the suitor, or if the young man was unwelcomed by the girl, mom and dad would "sit him out" until the wee hours.

- Do not share disagreements between you and your fiancé(e) with either set of parents.

- Do not go along with plans suggested by either parent just to keep the peace. Your dissatisfaction will eventually surface.

- Do not plan to live with either set of parents after the wedding unless it absolutely cannot be avoided.

Blending Your Families:
Reckoning with Relatives Respectfully

What to Do

- Decide as a couple that you will not let extended family issues come between you.

- Take time to develop a relationship with your new family members separate from your new spouse.

- Realize that you can't change other people, so don't try. You can only change yourself.

> "I told someone I was getting married, and they said, 'Have you picked a date yet?' I said, 'Wow, you can bring a date to your own wedding? What a country!'"
>
> Comedian Yakov Smirnoff

- Find ways to incorporate immediate family members into the wedding plans so they feel a part of the festivities.

- Take advantage of special skills or talents that family members have, but do not impose on people to help with the wedding just because they are family.

- Talk to your fiancé(e) about differences of opinion you may have with your new family. Perhaps he or she can explain their point-of-view, and that will help you see the problem differently.

- Let your in-laws know that you respect your soon-to-be spouse.

- Be creative in dealing with traits that bother you. For instance, if it annoys you that your future mother-in-law offers unwanted advice, make a preemptive strike by asking her advice on something that you know she is particularly knowledgeable about.

- Deal with issues that affect your family and let your fiancé(e) do the same.

Blending Your Families:
Reckoning with Relatives Respectfully

- Have the minister or another neutral party mediate if there is a major problem among family members.
- Remember to keep things in perspective. Planning the wedding is a highly emotional time for everyone, not just the bride and groom.
- Be honest when offering thoughts and ideas about your wedding.
- Present a united front about all decisions concerning the wedding.
- Thank your in-laws for their consideration with your plans and their efforts to fulfill them.
- Express respect to all family members in all your decisions.

> "Families are like fudge ...
> mostly sweet with a few nuts."
> — Unknown

What to Wear: All about Attire

What to Wear: All about Attire

Few details of the wedding are as obvious as the attire for the bride, her groom, and their attendants. Here are suggestions to ease the process of dressing everyone appropriately for the ceremony.

THE BRIDE

Almost every young girl imagines herself in her wedding dress long before she actually plans to be married. Choosing her dress is one of the most exciting parts of planning a wedding. Make sure to choose just the right one by considering the items below.

What NOT to Do

- Do not panic. There is an unlimited number of dresses to choose from, but a good consultant can help you find a starting place for your search.

- Do not go alone to shop for your wedding dress. Take your mother, a relative, or a trusted friend to offer an objective opinion.

- Do not agree to wear a dress you do not care for, whether it is a relative's dress offered for sentimental reasons, or a dress on sale at a too-good-to-be-true price.

> **Members of the Association of Wedding Gown Specialists, found in about 500 cities around the world, care for wedding gowns, old and new, with a specialty in heirloom gown preservation and vintage gown restoration. The Association also restores christening gowns, doll clothes, and table linens, many of which date back to the early 1800s.**

What to Wear: All about Attire

- Do not be afraid to choose an unusual style that you prefer. You want to like and feel good wearing your selection, so get something you want.

- Do not spend more than you are able to afford on your dress.

- Do not buy the first dress you see. You may regret an impulse purchase if you see something you like better later. Even if you find the same dress elsewhere, you may find it for a better price. You will never know until you shop around.

- Do not buy your dress based on a size you hope to be later. Be realistic. Dresses can be taken in fairly easily, but letting them out is much more difficult.

- Do not store your gown in a plastic bag before the big day. Fumes from the plastic could damage your gown.

What to Do

- Set a budget for the most you can afford and stick to it.

> The most photographed wedding dress in history is said to be the one worn by Jacqueline Bouvier, bride of John F. Kennedy. The dress required fifty yards of ivory silk taffeta and took more than two months to make. It was the creation of Ann Lowe, a native of Clayton, Alabama, whose ancestors were slaves.

- Figure in all items when estimating the cost of any dress you are considering. For instance, alterations may not be included, and may cost several hundred additional dollars.

- Also, consider accessories like gloves and shoes in your budget.

What to Wear: All about Attire

- Shop at a reputable store where consultants can help you choose a flattering style, and where someone is experienced in fitting.

- Wear appropriate under-garments when shopping for a dress. This will give you the truest idea of what your dress will look like on your big day.

- Ask friends for recommendations about the places they bought their dresses.

- Also ask friends for places you should avoid.

- Watch ads for sales of wedding dresses.

- Consider having your dress made for you if you know of an expert seamstress.

- Set aside enough time for shopping for your dress.

- Allow 8-12 weeks for delivery and fitting of your dress. Some deliveries can take several months.

> Match the length of your gown to the tone of the wedding you are planning. Full-length gowns are for formal weddings, shorter dresses are for informal ceremonies. The length of the veil should be in proportion to the length of the dress.

- Decide what color of dress you will wear. Although many brides still prefer traditional white, even delicate shades of pink, blue, ivory, and beige are frequent choices.

- Look through bridal magazines to see styles that you might like to try on. This can give you a starting place when you shop. It will be helpful for the salesperson to see a picture of the style you are looking for instead of trying to find it based on your description.

What to Wear: All about Attire

> Princess Diana's wedding attire included a second wedding dress, an exact replica of the one she was to wear, just in case the real one got damaged. The only difference between the dresses was the Queen Mary's lace sewn to the front of the one she wore; the replica had only a copy of the lace. The spare dress was recently sold at auction for $175,000.

- The silhouette of the dress is another factor to consider. Some dresses are more fitted, while others are looser, or have unusual lines. Here are some basic types you will find:

    - Princess and A-line dresses have side seams that run vertically from the underarm to the hem. These styles seem to be the most flattering.
    - Ball gowns are fitted at the waist but have full skirts. This style is the most traditional.
    - Sheaths are very fitted and highlight a trim figure, but you must measure carefully for them, and then hope your measurements do not change even slightly before the dress arrives.

    > In early Saxon times, poor brides came to their weddings dressed in plain white robes as a statement that she brought nothing with her to the marriage and, therefore, her husband was not responsible for her debts.

    - Mermaid shapes are fitted until they flare out below the knee.

What to Wear: All about Attire

- Empire dresses have high waistlines with a slender skirt flowing from a yoke seam just below the bust.

• If you choose to wear a veil, it should flatter your face, not overpower it. Here are some standard shapes of faces and the types of veils that suit them best:

- Oval faces can wear almost any style.
- Long faces may be softened by a band or wreath.
- Round faces can accommodate tiaras as well as bands and wreaths.

• Shoes should be traditional white or satin. Consider choosing closed-toe and heel styles to minimize worries about runs.

• Practice wearing your new shoes around your house. If they are smooth on the bottom, and slippery to walk in, scrape the bottoms with sandpaper or another rough substance to help minimize the risk of slipping.

> **If you plan to dance at your wedding reception, choose a veil that can be removed from the headpiece to facilitate your movement.**

> **When the wedding is over, be sure to preserve your wedding gown properly by making sure it is dirt/stain-free, and then packing it for long-term storage where it will not be subjected to extreme temperature, excess light, or insects.**

What to Wear: All about Attire

- Minimal jewelry should be worn with your wedding dress. A delicate choker or string of pearls may be worn on your neck, and your engagement ring is worm on your right hand until after the ceremony.

THE GROOM

Here is some help for the groom as he prepares to look special for his bride.

What NOT to Do

- Do not deal with a store that displays out-of-date styles and colors.

- Do not rent tuxedos from a store that does not have someone to measure you and your attendants.

- Do not be forced to accept the store representative's opinion about what you should select. If he or she insists on signing you up for their current special, run!

The tradition of a bride carrying a handkerchief originated because early farmers thought a bride's wedding day tears were lucky and brought rains for their crops. Later, a crying bride meant that she'd never shed another tear about her marriage. Today, we carry a handkerchief to dab away the tears of happiness and joy. Many brides keep their wedding handkerchief and pass it down to their daughter for use at her own wedding.

What to Wear: All about Attire

- Do not rent your tuxedo from anyone who cannot su[pply the] accessories you will need, such as a cummerbund o[r ...] somewhere that supplies everything at one place.

- Do not select something trendy that you will regret later. Traditional is always safer.

What to Do
- Decide how formal the wedding will be and shop accordingly.

- For the best selection, choose a formalwear store that regularly updates its inventory.

- Make your selection at least three months prior to the wedding.

- Select a style that suits your physique. For example, a heavyset person should not consider a double breasted jacket that will make him appear heavier.

- Coordinate your tuxedo with the color your bride has chosen for the wedding, as well as other details regarding style.

> The first documented marriage in Colonial America was in 1609 between Anne Burrows, a maid, and John Laydon, a carpenter, both of Virginia.

- Have your groomsmen get their tuxedos at the same shop as you get yours so there will be consistency in style and color.

- Ask out-of-town attendants to be measured in their town by a professional tailor, and then have the measurements sent to your shop.

- Call a week or two before the wedding to confirm details.

What to Wear: All about Attire

ick up tuxedos at the agreed-upon time, leaving time to settle small details that may need adjustment.

- Return all items on time with all pieces you were originally given.

ATTENDANTS

The attire of the attendants is chosen by the bride and groom, but here are some things to make it more pleasant for those in the wedding party.

What NOT to Do

- Do not select dresses or tuxedos without looking at the price tag. Money might not be an object for you, since you are creating a once-in-a-lifetime memory for yourself, but other people may be more cost conscious.

- Do not choose the dresses without considering which style will flatter the most body types.

- Do not order from a store that is inconvenient for your bridesmaids. Make it as easy as possible for them to be part of this special time.

What to Do

- Choose dresses that will flatter a variety of figures in order to accommodate the variety your bridesmaids may have.

- Consider allowing bridesmaids to choose non-identical styles to allow for individual fitting, though you will want to coordinate colors.

- Consider a two-piece outfit that offers different options for top and bottom to suit a variety of figures.

What to Wear:
All about Attire

- Select dresses whose color and design are appropriate for the season.

- Ask for input from your attendants since they will be the ones wearing the clothing you select.

- Keep in mind that your attendants will have other expenses besides their clothing when making a selection they will have to live with.

- Focus on the efforts your attendants are making for you and be gracious with any requests and suggestions they may make.

- Offer to provide and bear the expense for extras that you may want, such as particular necklaces to go with the dresses.

All That Glitters Is Not Gold: Rules for Rings and Things

All That Glitters Is Not Gold: Rules for Rings and Things

Here are some things that can help as you buy an engagement ring to symbolize your plans to marry, and then the wedding rings to symbolize your marriage.

BUYING AN ENGAGEMENT RING

Buying an engagement ring is an emotional experience, but it is also a big investment. Be sure you do your homework before you begin your search for this special gift.

What NOT to Do

- Do not spend so much on rings that you create a financial burden to live under as you begin your lives together.

- Do not shop alone. Shop together as a couple, or have a friend go along if you plan to surprise your intended with a ring. Two heads are better than one.

- Do not guess at the size ring you need. If it is to be a surprise, try to find out your girlfriend's ring size by taking one of her other rings with you for sizing.

- Do not allow yourself to be pressured into making a hasty decision about a ring.

The gimmal ring, made of three interlocking rings, originated during the Elizabethan period. During the engagement, the bride-to-be, the groom-to-be, and their witness each wore one of the rings until the wedding day, when the three pieces were united as a single ring for the bride.

All That Glitters Is Not Gold: Rules for Rings and Things

- Do not buy a diamond without having it independently appraised.
- Do not give a ring that you originally bought for someone else.
- Do not have a ring engraved without being sure it fits.
- Do not show others the ring before the intended bride sees it. She will want to be the one to show it off.

What to Do

- Determine your budget for the ring.
- Ask friends for recommendations about a jeweler you can trust.
- Be prepared to make basic decisions about whether you want modern or traditional bands, white or yellow gold, and whether you will each wear a band, or just the bride.
- Ask your jeweler for any printed material he might have on diamond-buying.
- Research important factors you should look for: color, cut, clarity, and carat. An additional consideration is cost.

As a safety measure, your jeweler can have a unique number laser inscribed in your diamond's outer edge. If you ever have it resized or cleaned, you can make sure you're getting your own diamond back by checking for the number. Your insurance company will no doubt appreciate this extra effort.

All That Glitters Is Not Gold: Rules for Rings and Things

Color – With the exception of fancy colored diamonds, the more colorless a diamond is, the higher its value. Jewelers grade diamonds on a scale from D (colorless) to Z (light yellow). Anything more yellow than D is considered fancy and is much more expensive. Here are some abbreviations used by jewelers to distinguish color:

D E F (colorless)

G H I J (near colorless)

K L M (faint yellow)

N O P Q R (very light yellow)

S T U V W X Y Z (light yellow)

Cut – This does not mean the shape of the diamond. It means how it is faceted to allow light to reflect from it. In a well-cut diamond, light enters it and reflects straight back to the viewer's eye.

Clarity – Diamonds frequently have inclusions, or small flaws, air bubbles, or scratches inside them. The fewer inclusions a diamond has, the more valuable it is. The scale for grading a diamond's clarity is:

– FL (flawless – no internal or external inclusions)

– IF (internally flawless – only slight external inclusions)

– VVS1-VVS2 (very, very lightly included – minute inclusions that even an experienced eye would find difficult to detect under 10x magnification)

– VS1 - V2 (very slightly inclusions invisible to the naked eye, and seen with difficulty under 10x magnification)

All That Glitters Is Not Gold: Rules for Rings and Things

- Sl1 - Sl2 (slightly included – invisible to the naked eye, yet easily seen by an experienced grader under 10x magnification)
- I1-I3 (included – inclusions are visible to the naked eye)

Carat – Refers to the size of the stone. Some prefer a large stone at the expense of other qualities, while some prefer a small stone regardless of their budget.

- Shapes to choose from include round, oval, marquise, square (princess), rectangular (emerald), pear, heart, and trillion (triangle).

- Know ahead of time whether your intended will want to be surprised by the presentation of a ring, or will want to participate in selecting it.

- If you intend the ring to be a surprise, there are many ways you can find out your loved one's preferences:

> The circular shape of the wedding ring has symbolized unending love since the early Egyptians wore rings made of hemp. Because they were not durable, they had to be replaced often. Iron was first used by the Romans for its durability. Now, gold is the metal of choice, for its beauty and purity.

- Examine rings that she already has to determine size, color of gold, and general style she prefers.
- Ask her friends for their opinions about her preferences.
- Make mental notes if she offers comments about rings her friends have received or about rings you have seen together.

All That Glitters Is Not Gold: Rules for Rings and Things

- If you buy the ring as a surprise, make sure you can exchange it if your fiancée prefers something else.

- Decide on a stone to purchase, whether it will be a traditional diamond, or some other favorite.

- Choose the setting after you decide on a stone.

- Choose the size of the ring in proportion to the size of the hand it will be on.

- Have the engagement ring insured.

- Keep your receipt for the ring.

- Store your receipt, appraisal, and other documents about the ring in a safe place.

- Have your jeweler inspect the ring on a yearly basis to be sure the stone(s) is secure.

> Some wedding superstitions say that once a bride's ring is placed on her finger by her groom, it must remain there at least until after the birth of their first child. If it accidentally comes off before then, the groom must be the one to replace it.

> The smallest engagement ring on record was given in 1518 to two-year-old Princess Mary, daughter of Henry VIII. The tiny gold band, which included a diamond, marked her engagement to the infant Dauphin of France, son of King Francis I.

All That Glitters Is Not Gold: Rules for Rings and Things

BUYING YOUR WEDDING RINGS

Your wedding rings will tell the world that you have made a commitment to each other. Make sure to get rings that you will be proud of for years to come by taking time to select them carefully.

What NOT to Do

- Do not buy the first rings you see. You may find something else later that you like better.

- Do not wait until the last minute to buy your rings. Allow plenty of time in case the rings you want have to be ordered or sized, and in case you choose to have them engraved.

- Do not have your rings engraved before you are sure they fit.

- Do not use rings worn by you or your fiancé(e) in a previous marriage.

What to Do

- Start looking early to get what you want at the best price.

- Shop around.

- Consider having your wedding date or a short message engraved in your rings to personalize them.

- Buy your wedding bands at the same time you buy the engagement ring to get a better price.

> In the early days of marriage by purchase, the betrothal ring served a twofold purpose. One was that it was partial payment for the bride. The other was that it was a symbol of the groom's honorable intentions.

All That Glitters Is Not Gold: Rules for Rings and Things

- Be sure your wedding bands match or are compatible with the engagement ring you choose.

- Choose rings with widths that will be comfortable to wear on a day-to-day basis.

> **When wearing a wedding and engagement ring on the same finger, the wedding ring goes on first (nearer the heart), followed by the engagement ring.**

- Look for marked jewelry. While it is not required by law that gold carry the karat marks defining its level or purity, virtually all reputable stores sell only marked gold. If it is karat-marked, it must be stamped with a hallmark, which shows that the manufacturer stands behind the karat mark's accuracy. The country of origin is also often noted. Here are some common karat indications.

24k	100 percent pure gold	So soft it is not often used for jewelry.
18k	75 percent gold, mixed with copper or silver	More "lemony" in tone, strong enough for rings.
14k	58.5 percent gold	Copper alloys make it durable, and give it a slightly reddish hue.
10k	41.6 percent gold	Less than 10-karat gold cannot be legally called or sold as gold in the US.

Decorating for the Ceremony: Featuring Flowers with Flair

Decorating for the Ceremony: Featuring Flowers with Flair

Flowers are a beautiful addition to wedding décor, as well as a lovely adornment for people in the wedding party. Make sure yours are chosen with care and consideration to enhance your ceremony.

What NOT to Do

- Do not wait until the last minute to book a florist to help you with your wedding. Most talented people are booked well in advance.

- Do not forget about your budget when planning your floral needs. Costs add up quickly unless you keep a running total as you plan.

> During Victorian times, lovers would send messages to each other using different flowers, with each flower having its own meaning. These associations were soon adopted for the bride's bouquets and are still used today by many brides.

- Do not try to choose a florist over the phone. You will not be able to make a good choice without meeting him or her in person.

- Do not settle on a florist without seeing samples of his or her work.

- Do not choose a florist that uses the same basic plan for every wedding.

- Do not work with a florist who is not receptive to your input.

> During Roman times, brides and grooms wore floral garlands to signify new life and hope for fertility.

- Do not be reluctant to ask for references.

Decorating for the Ceremony: Featuring Flowers with Flair

- Do not replace arrangements that are already at the wedding site with yours without getting permission to do so.

What to Do
- Enlist the help of a professional florist to help you plan which flowers you will use for your wedding.

- Ask friends and family members to recommend a florist they know and trust.

> The custom of the bride carrying flowers has its roots in ancient times. Strong smelling herbs and spices were thought to ward off and drive away evil spirits, bad luck, and ill health.

- Have some idea of the kinds of flowers you prefer and what you have in mind before you meet with a florist. Here are some other things you should finalize before your meeting.

    - Your primary color for the wedding
    - Where the wedding will be held
    - Arrangements appropriate for the site
    - Centerpieces needed for tables
    - Number of bridesmaids and the type of bouquet you want for them
    - Number of boutonnieres needed for groomsmen
    - Needs for the rehearsal dinner and reception
    - Corsages needed for mothers, grandmothers, musicians, and others involved

- Look through bridal magazines and surf the internet to get ideas about which flowers you would like to use, and how to arrange them.

Decorating for the Ceremony: Featuring Flowers with Flair

- Keep an open mind about options you may not have considered.

- Choose flowers suited to the season in which the wedding is held.

- Consider incorporating seasonal decorations that may already be at your wedding site into your plans. You can use the money you save for something else.

- Select flowers that will enhance the tone of your wedding. More elaborate arrangements would be appropriate for very formal weddings, while casual bouquets would be good for simpler ceremonies.

- Research the particular meanings of different flowers. This may help you select flowers appropriate for your purpose.

- Coordinate the color of your floral arrangements with your overall color scheme.

> "Flowers are love's truest language."
> Park Benjamin

- If you would like to keep the bridal bouquet as a memento, have the florist design a toss bouquet that can be thrown to eagerly awaiting bridesmaids.

- Make sure attendants carrying the flowers are not allergic to them.

- Find out when the wedding site will be available for decorating.

- Confirm all arrangements about a week before the wedding.

- Ask the church or hall where the wedding is held if they would like you to leave an arrangement for their next service or event.

- Arrange for your florist to store your bouquet as needed if you plan to have it preserved later.

Let Them Eat Cake: Conquering Catering Concerns

Let Them Eat Cake:
Conquering Catering Concerns

Your caterer will be in charge of food that your guests will enjoy at the reception. Here are some things to consider for this important part of the wedding.

What NOT to Do

- Do not settle on one caterer before you have compared several.

- Do not begin to meet with caterers before you have chosen a date for your wedding.

- Do not accept arrangements that you do not really want just because the caterer has done them before.

- Do not use a caterer who is not willing to accommodate your wishes.

- Do not choose a caterer based only on the lowest price quoted. Be willing to pay an appropriate amount for someone to serve your guests delicious food.

- Do not agree to having foods without taste-testing them first.

- Do not plan to serve foods that people will not recognize or be reluctant to try.

- Do not think you must accept a "standard" cake over a more creative one. Instead of a traditional bride and groom topper, you may use flowers, or even a miniature version of something that represents your favorite hobby.

- Do not plan to serve alcohol without checking to make sure that your reception location will allow it.

Let Them Eat Cake:
Conquering Catering Concerns

What to Do

- Begin your search for the right caterer as soon as you set your date.

- Check to see if a caterer may be on staff where you will have your reception. Even churches sometimes have someone in charge of overseeing their fellowship hall.

- When you talk with someone you are considering as your caterer, ask for names of people you may contact about their services.

- Check to see what facilities are available at your reception site before you meet with a potential caterer, so you can pass the information on to him or her.

- Ask if you may attend a function that a caterer is handling in the near future so you can observe his or her work personally. If that is not possible, ask to at least see what will be served before one of the caterer's events begins.

- Have the caterer plan to offer a variety of foods in order to have something all your guests will like.

- Be sure the caterer you choose carries basic liability insurance to cover any problems that arise.

> **Irish customs dictate that the wedding cake is cut by one of the bride's sisters or bridesmaids. The bride remains seated while groomsmen hold the cake over her head as it is cut.**

Let Them Eat Cake:
Conquering Catering Concerns

- Work with your caterer to get the wedding cake you want. Here are some things to consider:

    - White cake is traditional, but not mandatory. Choose a flavor that is your favorite.
    - Fillings can be as varied as the cake.
    - Consider using live greenery as decoration, but make sure it is not a poisonous variety.
    - Use your wedding color to highlight the cake.
    - Choose a seasonal cake, such as a spice cake for fall, or something light like lemon for summer.
    - Acknowledge your heritage by choosing an Italian cheesecake, an English pound cake, or another appropriate ethnic favorite.

- Find out about what portion of the money paid is refundable in the event of a change in plans.
- Confirm arrangements about a week before the wedding.

Picture This: Preparing for Perfect Photographs

Picture This:
Preparing for Perfect Photographs

Photographs from your wedding will be an enduring and cherished record of a special day in your life. Make sure you enlist just the right photographer to help you capture this day on film.

What NOT to Do

- Do not just take the word of other wedding service providers to help you choose your photographer. Other providers sometimes receive compensation for recommending those they work with regularly.

- Do not agree to purchase packages that you do not need or want.

- Do not try to pay for everyone's photos, though you may want to pay for parents' photos.

- Do not book a photographer on price alone. Even a rock-bottom price won't make up for poor quality pictures of this special day.

- Do not book your wedding based on a meeting with a salesperson. You deserve to meet and interview the person you will be trusting to capture your memories.

- Do not ask your photographer on the day of the wedding to take pictures that you have not agreed upon.

- Do not book any photographer without seeing samples of his or her work.

> "The ideal marriage is not one in which two people marry to be happy, but to make each other happy."
> — Roy L. Smith

Picture This:
Preparing for Perfect Photographs

- Do not allow friends and relatives to interfere with the photographer as he or she works by offering advice about who should be in each picture, or how they should be positioned.

- Do not allow photography or videography that will interfere with the wedding ceremony.

What to Do

- Plan to hire a professional photographer for your wedding.

- Start looking for the photographer as soon as you set a wedding date.

- Ask friends and relatives who have recently planned a wedding to recommend a photographer who they used or considered.

- Look through wedding albums of your friends to see the work of photographers they have used.

> Wedding photojournalism is the process of capturing special moments of the day as they happen, without posing them. This might include shots of the bride getting ready, a reluctant flower girl walking down the aisle, or the father of the bride giving his daughter away.

- Pay attention to any emotional response you have while looking at samples.

- Call for an appointment to discuss your plans with prospective photographers.

- Have some idea of what you want before you start to interview photographers.

Picture This:
Preparing for Perfect Photographs

- Know how much you can spend on the photographs and photographer.

- Be sure you and your photographer agree on how long he or she will stay at the wedding to make pictures. You do not want him or her to leave for another commitment before yours is finished.

- Book a photographer as soon as you set a date, especially if your wedding will be during a season common for weddings.

- Ask for references from photographers you are considering.

- Make sure the photographer you choose has a personality you can work with at the wedding. You may want to see him or her work at other weddings to observe interaction with the wedding party.

> The largest mass wedding in history occurred in Seoul in 1992 when Sun Myung Moon united 20,000 Unitarian couples on the same day. Another 9,800 attended and took their vows via satellite.

- Find out if the venue where you will have the wedding has restrictions on when and where photographs may be made.

- Let your prospective photographer know what type of photographs you hope to get, whether traditional or casual, standard poses, or something more creative.

- Specify whether you will want color photographs, black and white, sepia, or a combination.

- Ask to see additional albums besides the two or three that the photographer usually displays for viewing.

Picture This:
Preparing for Perfect Photographs

- Ask about the photographer's policy of allowing wedding guests to take pictures while formal pictures of the wedding party are being made.

- See if your photographer might also offer to have someone make a video of the wedding.

- Ask if the photographer develops the film in house, or if it is sent out. Outside labs may provide excellent pictures, but there is more risk of the film being lost during shipment.

- Try to negotiate the cost of your wedding package.

- Find out which services will cost extra.

- Ask how you will see proofs of your pictures — online or in hard copies.

- Once you have selected a photographer, get everything in writing. Details that should be included would be items such as these listed below.

    - Confirmation of the date
    - Time of arrival and departure
    - Package you have selected
    - Price
    - Number of color pictures
    - Number of black-and-white pictures, if any
    - Number of proofs you will receive
    - Whether proofs must be returned or may be kept
    - Couple's list of must-have photos

Picture This:
Preparing for Perfect Photographs

- List of pictures to be made with guests
- Information about any restrictions
- What kind of album will come with photos
- Provision for a refund if the wedding is canceled
- Terms of payment

- Be sure you understand what time the photographer will want the wedding party to be available for photographs.

- Confirm arrangements with your photographer several days before the wedding.

- Try to keep the photography session between the wedding and reception brief so that you do not keep guests waiting too long. Make sure refreshments are available during this delay.

> "A good snapshot stops a moment from running away."
> Eudora Welty

Melodies for Marriage: Making the Most of Your Music

Melodies for Marriage:
Making the Most of Your Music

Nothing helps set the appropriate tone for your ceremony more than beautiful and well-chosen music. Here are some suggestions to help your preparations be as smooth as your selections.

What NOT to Do

- Do not try to enlist musicians at the last minute. Not only might they already be booked, but they will need adequate time to prepare.

- Do not feel obligated to ask relatives to provide music if you prefer to use someone else.

- Do not ask musicians to be a part of your wedding without knowing the extent of their abilities.

- Do not expect musicians to participate in your wedding without being paid. Unless they indicate specifically that their service is a gift to you, be prepared to pay them for their preparation and performance time.

- Do not try to use music that is prohibited at your wedding location. Some churches request that no secular music be used. Others may ask that no instruments be used, only voices.

The Association for Wedding Professionals International is a central source of information and referrals for those planning weddings. Brides and grooms receive free referrals to wedding professional members who have agreed to operate under a code of ethics while offering their services.

Melodies for Marriage: Making the Most of Your Music

- Do not forget to thank musicians and soloists who help to make your ceremony special.

What to Do

- Identify what kind of music you will need, and when you will need it before you meet with a musician. Your needs might include these items.
    - Pre-service music, instrumental or vocal
    - Music at particular times during the service, for example, after a prayer
    - Music for seating special family members
    - Processional for attendants
    - Bridal march
    - Recessional for the wedding party
    - Background music for the reception
    - Dance music at the reception
- Select music appropriate to the tone of the ceremony. Classical music would be appropriate for a formal wedding and secular music for an informal one.
- Decide how many, at what point in the service, and who will sing songs that you wish to include in the ceremony.
- Let musicians know if they will need to prepare to accompany a soloist during the wedding so they can arrange to practice together.

> "The music at a wedding procession always reminds me of the music of soldiers going into battle."
> Heinrich Heine

Melodies for Marriage: Making the Most of Your Music

- Provide musicians and soloists with phone numbers of each other so they can make arrangements to work together.

- Get titles of your requested music, or better yet, copies of the musical scores, to the musicians as soon as possible.

- Ask musicians what special equipment they will need, such as extra microphones or CD players.

- Ask musicians what they will charge for their services. If you are using musicians provided by the wedding site, ask someone in the office about their policy on this.

- Enlist someone familiar with the sound system to operate it.

- Allow plenty of time for musicians and vocalists to prepare for the wedding.

- If you would like to include congregational singing, provide your guests with lyrics to the songs in your program, or display them where they can be seen.

- Arrange to have someone operate the site's video projection screen if lyrics to songs will need to be displayed.

- Check to see if musicians on staff at the wedding site are available for the service. For instance, if there is an organist at the church, he or she would be more familiar with that instrument than an outside musician would be.

- If you will not be using staff musicians, check to be sure that your musicians can obtain access to practice on the instruments they will be using.

Melodies for Marriage: Making the Most of Your Music

- Have musicians attend the rehearsal and practice with the wedding party to help set the timing of the music with the ceremony.

- Be sure to include musicians in the rehearsal dinner.

- Prepare a check and thank-you note to be given to the musicians at the conclusion of the ceremony. Some couples leave an envelope containing a check at the instrument or podium the musician will be using.

- Confirm arrangements with your musicians a week or so before the wedding.

Be Our Guest: The Ins and Outs of Invitations

Be Our Guest:
The Ins and Outs of Invitations

Your invitations are important messengers to your guests about the wonderful day you are planning. They will offer information about your big day, and if chosen carefully, will help set the tone for your ceremony. Make sure they are carefully prepared and sent by keeping the following suggestions in mind.

What NOT to Do

- Do not try to invite everyone you know to your wedding.

- Do not allow other people's issues to define your guest list. If there are people on your guest list who do not get along, that is their problem, not yours. Invite the people you want to.

- Do not retract invitations once they have been issued, unless, of course, the wedding has been called off.

- Do not use computer-generated address labels. Invitations should be addressed by hand. If your handwriting is not good, ask (or hire) someone to address the invitations for you.

> Statistics indicate the average number of people invited to a wedding to be 175.

- Do not send invitations out too late for people to make plans to attend.

> R.S.V.P. stands for the French phrase résponded s'il vous plaît (reply, please). If you include this in your invitation, do not add the word "please" because it is already included. It is acceptable to simply say, "please, reply."

Be Our Guest:
The Ins and Outs of Invitations

- Do not send response cards without stamps on them.

- Do not use vague terms such as "and guest" when addressing the inside envelope.

- Do not abbreviate titles such as "Doctor" and "Reverend."

- Do not hand-deliver invitations.

- Do not include information in the invitations about where the couple is registered.

- Do not put "cash only gifts" on the invitation even if that is what you prefer.

- Do not include children if you do not want to. Make sure to address the invitation to only those who are actually invited. It is not proper to put "No children" or "Adults only."

> It is a good idea to order extra envelopes in case you make errors in addressing them.

What to Do

- Determine early in your planning the size of your guest list. This will be an important number to know in making many of your plans.

- Make sure the style of the invitation is appropriate to the style of the ceremony to be held. For

> Informal postcard invitations may be sent if you are planning an informal wedding. Not only will this appropriately establish the tone for the ceremony to come, it will save money as opposed to an invitation sent in a sealed envelope.

Be Our Guest:
The Ins and Outs of Invitations

example, a very formal invitation would not be appropriate for a beach wedding.

- Spell out everything on the invitation, that is, use words to express the time of the day the ceremony will be held, not numerals.

- Use "requests the honor of your presence" when your wedding will take place in a church or religious setting. Use "requests the pleasure of your company" when it will not.

- Order invitations six to eight weeks before the date you plan to mail them.

- Include your wedding party members on your guest list. Of course they will already know the particulars of the event, but they may want an invitation to keep as a souvenir.

> **Tissue paper in invitations is a holdover from the days when it was needed to prevent the ink from smearing. Obviously, it is not needed today, and it is socially acceptable to omit it.**

- Prepare your list carefully, making sure to include these people.
    - Immediate families of the bride and groom
    - Grandparents of the bride and groom
    - Attendants
    - Spouses or dates of the attendants
    - Clergyman or officiant
    - Distant relatives
    - Professional acquaintances

Be Our Guest:
The Ins and Outs of Invitations

- Send "save the date" cards to alert guests to your date if you will be married at a time when calendars are likely to be full by the time invitations arrive.

- Ask to see proofs of the invitation before they are printed, and check them carefully for proper information. Be careful to check the spelling of dates and times.

- Make sure to spell names correctly on invitations.

- Let people know the date by which you will need their response card.

- Include directions to the wedding, or a map if the location will be hard to find for out-of-town guests.

> **Think about addressing these invitations! The record for the most wedding guests goes to V.N. Sudhakaran and N. Sathyalakshmi, who married in India in 1995. The marriage was witnessed by more than 150,000 people.**

- Enclose a printed R.S.V.P. card along with a stamped, self-addressed envelope to get a better response to your invitation.

- Include a travel card with information on airports, lodging, and transportation for destination weddings.

- Address the envelopes by hand.

> **Postage costs can be minimized by choosing a lightweight paper for your invitations, or cutting down on extras to be included, such as the second envelope.**

Be Our Guest:
The Ins and Outs of Invitations

- Write out full names of everyone invited when addressing the inside envelope.
- Write out full names when addressing the outer envelope.
- Use Roman numbers in names rather than "3rd" or "the third."
- Write out street, city, and state names when addressing envelopes.
- Use the address of the person(s) hosting the wedding as the return address on the outer envelope.
- Check the amount of postage needed for each invitation, and affix the proper amount.
- Mail invitations six to eight weeks before your wedding.
- Ask that your invitations be hand canceled at the post office.

Showers and Other Get-togethers: Pointers for Prenuptial Parties

Showers and Other Get-togethers: Pointers for Prenuptial Parties

No doubt, just before the wedding, you and your fiancé(e) will be honored by numerous parties, showers, and other social occasions. Here are some things your friends and family should consider when planning those special times.

What NOT to Do

- Do not think that showers and other celebrations cannot be hosted by family members. In the past, formal etiquette prevented this, but mores are more relaxed these days.

- Do not plan a shower without checking with the maid/matron of honor to see if she is planning something herself. Most experts agree that she should have the first opportunity to plan a shower if she would like to.

- Do not schedule the event too close to the wedding. That week or so just prior to the ceremony will already be crowded, so have your celebration before the last minute.

- Do not sponsor "selling" showers where guests see a demonstration of products and are then asked to buy them for the couple.

- Do not employ any theme or activities that would be embarrassing to the honoree or guests.

> **World Marriage Day, the second Sunday in February, honors husbands and wives as the basic units of society, and salutes "the beauty of their faithfulness, sacrifice, and joy in daily married life."**

Showers and Other Get-togethers: Pointers for Prenuptial Parties

- Do not try to invite everyone you know to this type of get-together. It should be a small, intimate affair so the bride can visit with all her guests.

- Do not invite people to the shower who will not be invited to the wedding.

- Do not invite the same people to several different parties. Limit each person to just a couple of events.

- Do not forget to invite people who live out of town. Even though they may not be able to come because of the distance, they would probably like the opportunity to send a gift, and would appreciate being included.

> **A good icebreaker activity for a shower is to take turns allowing each guest to state his or her name, and their relationship to the bride and groom.**

- Do not assign the bride or groom any responsibilities for the party. They have enough details to handle, and they should not be asked to help sponsor a party in their honor.

- Do not include information about where the couple is registered in the invitation. That should be passed along by word of mouth.

- Do not start the party without making sure everyone is introduced. Nametags may be helpful for this.

- Do not let guests leave without making sure you have a complete list of everyone in attendance matched up with the gift they brought.

Showers and Other Get-togethers: Pointers for Prenuptial Parties

What to Do

- Plan to have the shower or party several weeks before the wedding. There will be other things just prior to the big event, and you do not want the calendar to be too crowded.

- Decide if there will be a theme, such as a kitchen or lingerie shower.

- Be sure that the guest list includes members of the wedding party, the mothers of the bride and groom, sisters of each, and their closest friends.

- Include a map or directions to the location for the shower when invitations are mailed.

- Send invitations far enough in advance to allow guests to make plans to come and to select an appropriate gift.

- Indicate in the invitation the type of gift that will be appropriate (lingerie, kitchen item, etc.).

- Offer sizes and colors for possible gifts when necessary.

- Make sure the bride and groom are registered for items they need so guests will know what to select.

Wedding breakfasts are often hosted by friends of the bride or groom in honor of all those who have come from out of town for the occasion. Neither the bride, groom, nor their families are expected to attend, but it is a good way to entertain and welcome guests who are away from home.

Showers and Other Get-togethers: Pointers for Prenuptial Parties

- Check with the bride and/or groom before finalizing the guest list and sending invitations.

- Keep the menu and activities simple. You do not want to spend the time making sure that complicated plans are carried out, only to find later that you have missed all the fun.

- Acknowledge gifts with thank-you notes as soon as possible.

- Thank the hostess(es) for having planned the event.

Setting up Housekeeping: Getting Gifts Graciously

Setting up Housekeeping: Getting Gifts Graciously

Receiving gifts for your new home together is one of the fun parts of getting married. Remember these courtesies as you are showered with gifts by your friends and family.

GIFT REGISTRY

A registry can help take the frustration and guesswork out of buying wedding gifts. Here are some things the couple should remember when selecting items to be included.

What NOT to Do

- Do not register for things you do not need, thinking you will return them for cash. List only items that you truly need.

- Do not register at stores where there is not a flexible return policy.

- Do not register for the same things at different stores.

- Do not register more than six months before the wedding. Statistics show that most gifts are bought within days of being given. Also, because of inventory turnover, something you register for today may not be available months later.

For a unique wedding memento, contact the Greetings Office in Washington, DC, to request a special message from the president of the United States. Wedding greetings must be requested after the event, and will be sent in response to those who qualify according to guidelines listed at www.whitehouse.gov/greeting.

Setting up Housekeeping: Getting Gifts Graciously

- Do not include registry cards with your wedding invitations. They may be provided with more informal shower invitations.

- Do not register for so many things that gift-givers are overwhelmed by pages of printed-out registry information at the store.

- Do not intentionally pick out the most expensive items for your registry.

- Do not be reluctant to register for a few expensive items. Having a few higher priced gifts will offer people the option of going together for a group gift.

- Do not include "No Gifts" on your invitations. If you and your fiancé(e) already have established homes and do not need help setting up housekeeping, relay this information by word-of-mouth instead.

- Do not tell people if they give you a gift you have already received.

- Do not use wedding gifts until after the wedding.

What to Do

- Register for gifts soon after you announce your engagement.

- Select where you will register for gifts you need.

- Choose items that you will need for your new life together.

- Register at several stores to make it more convenient for all your guests.

> "Marriage is a book of which the first chapter is written in poetry and the remaining chapters in prose."
>
> Beverly Nichols

Setting up Housekeeping: Getting Gifts Graciously

- If you already have all the household items you need, consider putting together a honeymoon registry so people can contribute toward something special that you might not otherwise be able to enjoy.

- Register for items from a variety of price ranges. Some gift-givers may need modestly-priced suggestions, while groups, such as co-workers, may welcome a higher ticket item that they can buy jointly.

THANK-YOU NOTES

Gifts should be acknowledged as soon as possible after receipt of the gift. Other courtesies to be remembered include those listed below.

What NOT to Do

- Do not forget to send notes to people who helped plan your wedding and events surrounding it.

- Do not mention the dollar amount of gift cards you received in your thank-you, but do mention what you plan to use them for.

- Do not think that because a gift came from a family member, no thank-you note is necessary. Send a note to every gift-giver, no matter what their relation to you.

> The world's most expensive wedding reportedly took place in 1981 between Sheik Rashid Bin Saeed Al Maktoum's son and Princess Salama in Dubai at a cost of more than $44 million.

- Do not let a long period of time elapse before sending thank-yous.

Setting up Housekeeping: Getting Gifts Graciously

- Do not write the note from just one person. Make sure to acknowledge the gift to the couple.

What to Do

- Order formal thank-you notes to match your invitations. If you prefer something more informal, these can be purchased at card shops or department stores.

- Show your gratitude for the gifts you received by sending thank-you notes.

- Send individual thank-you notes to each person who contributed to a group gift if there were less than ten people to give it. For larger groups, such as with an office gift, write one thank-you card and post it in a visible location. Thank the givers individually in person when you see them.

- Handwrite thank-you notes. Do not type them.

The longest marriage on record was between Taiwan's Liu Yung-yang and his wife, Yang-wan, who were married eighty-six years before her death in 2003. Though they married in 1917 in their late teens, they had lived under the same roof since Yang-wan had been sent to live with her future husband's family at the age of five. Following the custom of poor Taiwanese families, she joined her intended's family to take care of him and to do household chores.

Setting up Housekeeping: Getting Gifts Graciously

- Write thank-yous on note cards, not on cards with pre-printed messages. The message should be written by you, not pre-printed over your signature.

- Make reference at which occasion the gift was received if it was at a shower or get-together.

- Mention the specific gift that you received from each person.

- Include something in your note about how the gift will be used.

- If the giver of the gift was unable to attend the wedding, mention how sorry you were that he or she could not be there for the occasion.

- Include a wedding snapshot for people who may not have been able to attend.

- Acknowledge all gifts, even if you do not especially care for them. At least you can thank the giver for his or her thoughtfulness.

- Send a separate thank-you note for each gift, even though several gifts may have come from the same person.

- It is a thoughtful gesture to also send thank-you notes to the vendors who helped with your wedding.

Let's Call the Whole Thing Off: Canceling With Consideration

Let's Call the Whole Thing Off: Canceling With Consideration

If you or your fiancé(e) decide that the marriage is not the right thing for any reason, do not hesitate to call off your plans. Here are some suggestions to help you through this difficult, but sometimes appropriate, decision.

What NOT to Do

- Do not hesitate to cancel your plans if you feel that the marriage is not the right thing to do.

- Do not force yourself to go through with the plans just because people expect it, or because deposits have been paid.

- Do not think you are the only person to ever cancel a wedding. You aren't the first, and you won't be the last.

- Do not just fail to show up for the wedding. Let people know that you have changed your mind.

- Do not feel you have to explain or apologize to people about your decision.

- Do not worry what people will think about your decision.

> **If you feel that the wedding should be called off, do not hesitate to do so. You will not be alone. It is estimated that about 15 percent of couples who plan to marry end up calling off the wedding.**

- Do not speak poorly about your ex if you do not go through with the marriage.

- Do not casually discuss reasons for your decision with others.

Let's Call the Whole Thing Off: Canceling With Consideration

> **Wedding insurance protects you against financial losses you may incur in the event of unpredictable situations, such as serious illness or severe weather, during the period leading up to and including your wedding day. It may not, however, protect you if you or your intended cancel the wedding because you have changed your mind.**

- Do not be reluctant to lean on friends for support during this time of change.

What to Do

- Let everyone involved know of the change in plans as soon as possible.

- Cancel reservations made with venues for the wedding and reception.

- Send printed cards to let guests know about the change, or make phone calls if time is short. A printed notice might read something like this:

>Mr. and Mrs. Tony Jones
>announce that the marriage of their daughter
>Jamie to Mr. Chad Robert Smith
>has been canceled.

Let's Call the Whole Thing Off: Canceling With Consideration

- Offer an explanation only if the wedding is being postponed, not cancelled, due to sickness or other circumstances that cannot be helped. Wording used might be similar to this:

> Mr. and Mrs. Tony Jones
> regret that they are obliged to recall
> the invitations to the marriage of their daughter
> Jamie Lynn to Mr. Chad Robert Smith
> due to the death of Mr. Smith's father,
> Robert Earl Smith

To "have cold feet," meaning to back out of some undertaking because of anxiety about it, is an expression that has been around at least since Ben Johnson used it in his 1605 play <u>Volpone</u>. Some accounts say the term originally referred to a soldier whose feet were very cold, and who could, therefore, only proceed slowly or not at all.

- Ask family members to help make phone calls so you are not questioned about your decision while on the phone.
- Let out-of-town guests know first so they can change their travel plans as soon as possible.
- Return gifts that have not been used.

Let's Call the Whole Thing Off: Canceling With Consideration

- Add a note to returned gifts thanking the giver for the gift, but indicating that you felt that you should return it since the wedding has been canceled.

- The engagement ring should be returned to the groom, as well as other personal items given for the impending marriage. If the groom has called off the marriage, perhaps the bride may be entitled to keep the ring, but the classiest thing is to return it. Besides, if it is kept, it would only serve as a reminder of a heartbreaking experience.

- Cancel honeymoon reservations.

- Check with vendors to see if orders placed can be canceled, if deposits are partially refundable, or what your financial obligations are.

- Allow yourself time to adjust to the change in plans.

- Send a new invitation later if the wedding is only postponed, and not canceled.

Now I Pronounce You: Conducting the Ceremony Correctly

Now I Pronounce You: Conducting the Ceremony Correctly

All your work and planning is leading up to the big day, the centerpiece of which will be the wedding ceremony. Make sure yours is perfect by observing the items below.

What NOT to Do

- Do not panic if some details go awry. Focus on the big picture.

- Do not omit elements that you would like to include just because they are not traditional. This is your day and it should be tailored to your preferences.

- Do not move furniture or other items in the church or hall without asking permission from someone in charge.

- Do not try to direct your wedding yourself. Enlist an organized and experienced person to do this for you.

- Do not be late in starting the service.

- Do not embarrass your guests with an overly-zealous kiss at the end of the ceremony.

Looking for something different for your wedding? **Weird Weddings** is the name of a documentary television series that seeks to show North American couples "tying the knot in interesting and unusual ways." The program is no longer being filmed, but airs on the Women's Entertainment Network in the USA, and on the Life network in Canada.

Now I Pronounce You: Conducting the Ceremony Correctly

What to Do

- Select a location for the ceremony as early in your planning as possible, especially if you will be married near a holiday or other special occasion. Many venues are booked months in advance during such times.

- Choose a minister, rabbi, or judge to perform the ceremony.

- Meet with the officiant before the ceremony to discuss the type of service you and your fiancé(e) want.

- Schedule and attend pre-marital counseling if it is required by your church or minister.

- Decide whether you will follow traditional seating (with guests of the bride on the left, and groom's on the right), or open seating. Advise ushers accordingly.

- Indicate where special family members will sit by roping off sections to be used.

- Have all participants arrive early enough to make photographs, and take care of other preliminaries that must be done before the ceremony.

In times when women were granted few privileges and even fewer personal rights, the bride was literally given away to the groom by the father, usually in exchange for monetary gain. Today, it is seen as symbolic of the blessings and support of the union.

Now I Pronounce You: Conducting the Ceremony Correctly

- Check with the church or synagogue ahead of time to see if there are guidelines to be followed on your choice of music or other portions of the service.

- Arrange to have adequate dressing space for the wedding party at the wedding site.

- Incorporate religious and cultural elements of the bride and the groom in the ceremony.

- Consider sharing the cost of flowers and other amenities if there is to be another wedding at the same venue on the same day.

- If you are planning an outdoor wedding, have an alternative location just in case there is bad weather.

> In ancient wedding ceremonies, it was customary for the father of the bride to take one of the bride's shoes from her foot and present it to the groom as a symbol of transferring authority over the bride. The groom then tapped the bride on the head with the shoe to signal recognition of the transfer.

- Schedule a rehearsal of the ceremony a day or so before the wedding. Go through every aspect of the ceremony so everyone knows what to expect and when.

- Decide ahead of time how you will want your wedding party to process. A common sequence is as follows:

    - Mother and grandmothers of the bride and groom are seated.
    - The officiant takes his or her place at the altar.
    - The groom takes his place in front of the officiant.

Now I Pronounce You: Conducting the Ceremony Correctly

- The best man enters.
- Bridesmaids and groomsmen enter together or separately.
- The maid/matron of honor enters.
- The ring bearer and/or flower girl enter.
- The bride enters with an escort if she has one.

- Invite all those involved in rehearsal, plus their dates or spouses, to the rehearsal dinner.

- Consider providing a nursery area for children during the ceremony so that an infant's cry or a toddler's talk does not interrupt the service.

> A 2003 survey shows the median age of first marriages in the United States to be 27.1 for males and 25.3 for females.

- Rope off seats to be reserved for special family members.

- Let ushers know whom they should seat in the designated areas.

- Decide with your director on an order of service for the wedding. A typical service usually follows this general outline:

  - Pre-wedding music
  - Processional
  - Opening words from the officiant
  - Prayer
  - Giving the bride away
  - Comments about marriage
  - Vows

Now I Pronounce You: Conducting the Ceremony Correctly

- Special reading or song
- Exchange of rings
- Lighting of the unity candle
- Closing
- Declaration of marriage
- Introduction of the newlyweds
- Recessional

> In Greece, brides may carry a lump of sugar in their gloves to ensure a "sweet life."

- Offer printed programs for the guests so they may follow along with the ceremony. Besides being useful, they make wonderful keepsakes.

    - Include the names of all participants, even those not in the actual ceremony, such as the decorator or the planner.
    - Add an appropriate verse or design symbolizing your sentiments on the cover.
    - Coordinate the color of the program to your wedding theme.
    - Mention any absent family members who helped with the ceremony but are unable to attend.
    - Print lyrics to songs to be used if guests will join in the singing. Be sure to get permission for reprinting the words if the songs are protected by copyright.
    - Consider using a picture of the couple for the cover of the program.

- Order extra copies of the program for keepsakes.
- Display the programs so guests may take one as they enter, or ask ushers to help distribute them.

Receiving Your Guests: Recipe for a Ritzy Reception

Receiving Your Guests: Recipe for a Ritzy Reception

Your reception will be the first social occasion you and your new spouse will enjoy together as a married couple. Make sure all the details are perfect for you and your guests by taking the following items into consideration as you prepare.

CHOOSING A SITE

The most basic part of a good reception is choosing the correct location for it. It should be big enough to comfortably hold all of your guests, and should offer adequate room for all the activities you plan for your celebration.

What NOT to Do

- Do not wait too late to get the venue you want for your reception. Some places are booked as much as a year in advance.

- Do not start looking for a site until you know how many people to expect. Then you will know how much space you need.

- Do not choose a site that will not offer adequate room for the number of guests you will have.

Garter-throwing comes from a bawdy British ritual called "flinging the stocking." Guests would playfully invade the bridal chamber. The ushers would grab the bride's stockings; the maids would take the groom's. They took turns sitting at the foot of the bed flinging the stockings over the heads of the couple. Whoever's stocking landed on the bride's or the groom's nose would be the next to wed.

Receiving Your Guests:
Recipe for a Ritzy Reception

- Do not choose a site that will not accommodate your plans: If dancing will be part of the festivities, make sure you have room to allow it.

- Do not sign any agreement about any location unless you understand clearly what you are signing.

> **The tradition of tying tin cans to the bumper of newlyweds' cars originated when items which could produce noise were tied to the back of a couple's carriage to scare away evil spirits.**

What to Do

- Unless the location for your ceremony will have an adjoining reception hall, begin thinking early about where your reception will be held.

- Consider hotels, clubs, restaurants, mansions, public gardens, and parks as possible sites.

- Choose a site that will accommodate any special needs that your guests may have.

- Take into account how many tables you will need to comfortably accommodate your guests, and allow space accordingly.

> **In Bermuda, wedding cakes are often topped with a tiny sapling, which newlyweds plant at their new home and watch grow, symbolizing the growth of their marriage.**

- Decide as early as possible what your overall theme will be, and make sure your reception location is suitable.

Receiving Your Guests:
Recipe for a Ritzy Reception

- Check for adequate lighting at any location you are considering.

- Find out what services the hall staff will offer, and how the personnel will interact with the caterer and other service people you have chosen.

- Ask how rates for the event will be calculated, what additional charges might be added, and why.

- If a deposit is required, check to see if it will be deducted from the final bill, or returned, assuming that there are no damage or breakage charges.

- Be sure you understand exactly what is included in the services you agree upon.

- Check to see that the site offers a guaranteed-date policy so you are not bumped for a larger party.

> Throwing rice has always been a symbol of wishing prosperity and good luck. In the Orient, throwing rice means you wish the couple to always have a full pantry.

- Know ahead of time what tips and gratuities are expected of any staff involved in your reception.

- Find out exactly when you will have access to the hall for set-up and decorating.

Receiving Your Guests: Recipe for a Ritzy Reception

ENJOYING THE CELEBRATION

The pressure is off, and now you can celebrate. Have a great time greeting your guests as you receive their warm wishes for your new life.

What NOT to Do

- Do not keep your guests waiting for an unreasonable period of time while you make pictures.

- Do not drink so much that you cannot enjoy or remember the celebration.

> Cutting the wedding cake together, a tradition still observed at most receptions, symbolizes the couple's unity and their new life together as one.

- Do not spend so much time with some guests that you are unable to greet others.

- Do not make extended toasts.

- Do not seat guests together who you know do not care for each other.

- Do not seat guests near loud music if you know they will be bothered by it.

- Do not leave leftover food for people at the reception site to deal with.

What to Do

- Offer immediate seating to those who may be unable to work through a receiving line, or go through a buffet.

Receiving Your Guests: Recipe for a Ritzy Reception

- Consider any special needs your guests may have such as dietary restrictions or disability aids.

- Make sure guests at the ceremony receive clear instructions on how to get to the reception hall. Ministers often handle this by explaining to the congregation the way to the church's fellowship hall after the wedding party has recessed.

- Try to visit with as many guests as possible and thank them for coming.

- If you have a formal receiving line, be sure to include these people:
    - Mother of the bride
    - Mother of the groom
    - Bride
    - Groom
    - Maid/matron of Honor
    - All of the bridesmaids

- Fathers of the bride and groom may also be included, but may also stand nearby in a more casual role.

- Create your own arrangement for the receiving line if family circumstances dictate, for instance, if a mother of either the bride or groom is deceased.

- Seat dinner guests by age or by their relationship to the couple.

- Arrange guests to make it easier for them to visit together. For example, round tables allow all guests to see and talk with each other better than longer ones.

Receiving Your Guests: Recipe for a Ritzy Reception

- Have the caterer pack a goodie bag for you to take when you leave in case you are so busy greeting guests that you don't get to eat during the reception.

- Before you allow guests to throw rice as you leave, check to be sure it is allowed. Some venues request that you use birdseed instead because birds are often harmed by eating rice.

- Offer mementoes of your wedding to guests as they leave. A variety of novelty items can be imprinted with the couple's names and the date.

- Make sure someone takes charge of items that should be saved for you, such as the wedding topper and the top layer of the cake, which you'll freeze and enjoy on your first anniversary.

Getting Away from It All: Honeymooning Without Hassles

Getting Away from It All: Honeymooning Without Hassles

After all the excitement and stress of a wedding, you can look forward to time alone with your new spouse on your honeymoon. You can have a wonderful time if you are willing to invest a little effort into researching and planning your dream trip. Here are some guidelines that may be of help.

What NOT to Do

- Do not wait until the last minute to make your arrangements.

- Do not forget about passports, visas, or shots that you will need for overseas travel.

- Do not let yourself be talked into a trip that you do not want, simply because it is a bargain.

- Do not be reluctant to ask your travel agent details about the trip. You deserve to know what to expect.

> Statistics show that couples spend three times the amount on a honeymoon than they would spend on a regular vacation.

- Do not go into debt for a trip that you cannot afford.

- Do not rely on your memory for packing for your trip. Make lists to help you be organized. With all the pre-wedding activity, there is no way you will remember everything.

- Do not duplicate toiletries that you will need. Now is a good time to begin to share.

- Do not forget the basics like medications and sunscreen. They will no doubt be more expensive at your destination.

Getting Away from It All: Honeymooning Without Hassles

- Do not leave on your trip without giving a trusted friend or family member information about how you can be reached in the event of an emergency.

- Do not forget your camera. You will want to take pictures to record your trip.

What to Do

- Determine your overall budget for your trip, including travel, spending money, and meals, if they are not included.

- Include gratuities as you calculate how much money you will need.

- Talk with your fiancé(e) about a destination you would both enjoy.

- Check the internet and travel magazines for destination ideas.

- Think about going somewhere neither of you have been, and then enjoy the pleasure of discovering it together.

- Check with travel agents for the best prices.

- Consider setting up a honeymoon registry so people can give you portions of your trip as a gift.

- Include luggage and other travel items you need in your registry.

> "What a happy and holy fashion it is that those who love one another should rest on the same pillow."
> Nathaniel Hawthorne

- Consider all-inclusive packages which provide food, activities, and accommodations for a flat price.

- Make your reservations well in advance to get the best price.

- Be sure you understand all arrangements included in your plans.

Getting Away from It All: Honeymooning Without Hassles

> Why is the wedding trip called a honeymoon? In ancient times, when men captured their brides, they carried them off to a secret place where her relatives couldn't find them. While the moon went through all its phases (about thirty days), they hid from the searches and drank a brew made from honey. Hence, honeymoon.

- Ask about cancellation policies, inclement weather provisions, etc.

- Allow ample time for travel in planning your itinerary.

- Make sure to allow time for relaxation. Do not schedule an activity for every minute you are away.

- Let the people where you'll be staying know you'll be on your honeymoon. They may offer a special rate, or extra services to make your visit special.

- Confirm all arrangements the week of the wedding.

- Even if the bride is changing her last name when she marries, it may be easier to keep all her travel documents under her maiden name, and then change them when there is time after the trip.

- Take along a copy of your marriage certificate to answer questions that may arise about discrepancies in names on documents. Although you may not receive your official certificate until several weeks later, the minister may give you one to suffice in the meantime.

- Arrange for someone to get your mail, see about pets, and take over other household routines while you are away.

- Allow for time to wind down from the trip when you return.

Tying up Loose Ends: Finishing with Finesse

Tying up Loose Ends: Finishing with Finesse

After all the excitement has died down, there still remain a few details to take care of. Be sure to finish everything you started by following these guidelines.

What NOT to Do

- Do not let much time go by without finishing your thank-you notes.

- Do not keep wedding proofs beyond the time allotted.

- Do not fail to return dishes or utensils used at the reception.

> Digital photography now makes it possible for friends and relatives to view your wedding proofs online. They are usually placed on a website bearing the photographer's name, and then users click on the couple's name to see their proofs.

- Do not forget to retrieve all personal items from the wedding site.

- Do not keep borrowed or rented items used during the wedding. Return them to their owner by the designated time.

- Do not be surprised if you experience a letdown after the wedding. Accept this as a normal part of a big event in your life, and realize that it will pass.

What to Do

- Have someone put the bridal bouquet in a cooler, or take it to the appropriate person if it will be dried to preserve it.

- Freeze the top layer of your wedding cake so you can enjoy it on your first anniversary.

Tying up Loose Ends: Finishing with Finesse

> So you think Britney Spears had the shortest marriage on record? In 1919, Rudolph Valentino and Jean Acker wed and then split up six hours later when the bride locked the movie legend out of their honeymoon suite. He gave up and left, though they weren't legally divorced until 1922.

- Take the bridal dress to be properly stored, or return it to where you borrowed or rented it.
- Check with the photographer to see when proofs will be ready for viewing.
- Make sure all family members have a chance to see the photographs.
- Coordinate orders for photographs from family members and turn them in to the photographer on time.
- Collect any disposable cameras used and have them developed.
- Send change-of-address forms to let everyone know of your new address.
- Pay all outstanding balances due to vendors.
- Send thank-you cards to everyone who helped with your wedding.
- Open gifts received since the wedding.
- Acknowledge every gift sent.
- If the bride will take the husband's last name, find out how that can be done. Procedures vary by state, but here are some general guidelines for making the change.

Tying up Loose Ends: Finishing with Finesse

- Get a copy of your marriage license. Get two or three certified copies from the office where you applied for the license. You will need to show this document several times as proof of your name change. A photocopy may suffice, but have extras on hand just in case.

- Change your driver's license by going to the Department of Motor Vehicles in person and showing your marriage license. Some states offer the option to change your voter registration there as well.

> **The American suffragist Lucy Stone (1818-1893) was one of the first women in the United States to continue to use her own last name after marriage instead of assuming her husband's. As a result, women who choose not to take their husband's names are sometimes referred to as Lucy Stoners.**

- Change your Social Security card by going to the Social Security Office in your area and taking along a certified copy of your marriage license. You will probably need another form of identification showing your name, but if you've already changed your driver's license, this will suffice. The Social Security Administration should notify the IRS and Post Office, so you will not have to contact these places separately. Also, check to see if you can download a form for this online.

- Banks will probably only need to see a photocopy of your marriage license in order to change your name on accounts. They may also need a letter stating your intention to change

Tying up Loose Ends:
Finishing with Finesse

> The custom of the groom carrying his bride over the threshold when they enter their home for the first time after their marriage began when grooms captured their brides and carried them by force to their homes. Another version of this tradition says it was based on the belief that family demons that followed a bride could not go with her inside her new home if she was carried across the threshold the first time. After that, the demons could never enter.

your name, but check with your own bank for the particulars. Don't forget to order new checks with your new name, too.

- Change your passport by mailing in a certified copy of your marriage license, along with an application to the appropriate passport center. You can get copies of this application at the post office. If you are only changing your name, and not renewing your passport, there may be no charge.

- Let your local government offices know so they can bill local services such as water and garbage to your new name, as well as include it correctly if you have a city directory.

- Let your employer know of the change so your wages will be reported correctly, and you will not have any problems taking advantage of your benefits. Have new business cards printed if needed.

- Make the change in your credit and debit cards by calling customer service numbers provided by the institution issuing the cards.

Tying up Loose Ends: Finishing with Finesse

- Add each other's names to other important documents, including these listed below.
  - IRAs and CDs
  - Stocks and bonds
  - Safe deposit box
  - Loans
  - Insurance policies
  - Wills
  - Property titles
  - Leases

> "Chains do not hold a marriage together. It is threads, hundreds of tiny threads which sew people together through the years."
> Simone Signoret

If You Liked *What NOT to Do at Your Wedding!*, You'll Enjoy Other Books in This Series

ISBN: 1-58173-360-7
$7.95
What NOT to Say! is an indispensable guide to words and phrases that are often mispronounced, misspelled, and misused.

ISBN: 1-58173-318-6
$7.95
What NOT to Name Your Baby! can help you choose a name for your child that will be a blessing instead of a burden.

ISBN: 1-58173-405-0
$7.95
What NOT to Do in Polite Company! addresses personal and professional etiquette issues specific to our culture.

ISBN: 1-58173-408-5
$7.95
What NOT to Do at Work! will help you treat your co-workers, boss, and clients with the respect and courtesy they want and deserve.